A
speaking with grackles by subjects...

César Leonardo de Leon's poems are elemental gifts that ground us at once in the beauty of the Rio Grande Valley land and its seemingly steady assurances while also taking flight like kites and kestrels. As the collection progresses, silences mount and unravel in conditions created by toxic masculinities, inequities, and US American empire: "everywhere / the swallowing of huizache / thorns / labeled apple pie." de León's poems speak from those silences in powerful poems that celebrate lucecitas and rascuachismo and mourn the lives lost to militarized borderlands, mass shootings, police brutality, and COVID. An admirable debut collection by an outstanding poet.

—Emmy Pérez, Texas Poet Laureate 2020,
author of the poetry collections *With the River on Our Face*

César Leonardo de Leon's first collection glows with the immediacy of a cultural pastoral —lush in its ambitions and profuse in its design as it wrestles with South Texas. It both embraces and rejects Mexican-American identity— happily housed there and eager to leave. I marveled at the nimble imagery that challenges machismo, racism, tradition, and violence in these pages: "Every man for his own / myth and monolith anchored /around their collar". I marveled at the way de León finds poetry in the pork belly of boiled beans and the mariposas of the delta, wearing nature as a fine gown: "the summer of cat's claw and yucca thickets / diagraming names / of future lovers / threaded / through chain-link fences / each a constellation of open windows". I marveled at how a lover is described with "the cinnamon birthmark that migrated / north / con las mariposas" and a ghost flower reflects on how "something surviving / in this body yearns for river". The last poem in the collection asks, "don't you recognize me, america?" and the answer is clearly no, because a new original voice has arrived, one that demands attention. An impressive debut.

—Rodney Gomez, Poet Laureate of McAllen, Texas
and author of *Arsenal with Praise Song*

Firm and defiant in its claim to the literal and figurative Borderlands, this sumptuous poetry collection welcomes the reader into a world rich with the ways we create meaning from the muddy banks of our lives. A fierce debut. How fortunate we are to experience this new voice in poetry.

—José Antonio Rodríguez, author of *This American Autopsy*

speaking with grackles by soapberry trees is a masterpiece. César Leonardo de Leon's poetry here is a whole universe lit up by el sol and la luna at the same time. de Leon cuts straight to the bone with such precision, imagery and lyricism one can not bear to put the book down. César takes you to the edge of the river, knotting you up in the throat and the heart and leaves you in new lands you never dreamed of. These poems are lyrical, they are decadent, they are bittersweet, they are real life. de Leon provides you a new landscape honoring all things queer, bordered, forgotten, and desired. César warns and wishes in these poems, he invites you to a remarkable space, where "here a hummingbird can dream of being king." We dream with him every time we read this work.

—Lupe Mendez, 2022 Texas Poet Laureate, author of *Why I Am Like Tequila* (Willow Books, 2019)

SPEAKING WITH GRACKLES
BY SOAPBERRY TREES

FLOWERSONG
PRESS

BY CÉSAR LEONARDO DE LEÓN

FLOWERSONG
PRESS

FlowerSong Press
Copyright © 2021 by César Leonardo de León
ISBN: 978-1-953447-72-2
Library of Congress Control Number: 2021941812

Published by FlowerSong Press
in the United States of America.
www.flowersongpress.com

Cover Art by Nicol Bowles
Cover Design by Priscilla Celina Suarez
Set in Adobe Garamond Pro

No part of this book may be reproduced without written permission from the Publisher.

All inquiries and permission requests should be addressed to the Publisher.

ACKNOWLEDGMENTS

Thank you to the following publications where some of the poems included were first published, sometimes in slightly different forms. *Pilgrimage, Queen Mob's Tea House, La Bloga: Online Floricanto, FEIPOL: Antología Official de Poetas Participantes, Lost: Children of the River, The Border Crossed Us: An Anthology to end Apartheid, Pulse/Pulso: In Remembrance of Orlando, No Tender Fences: An Anthology of Immigrant & First-generation American Poetry, Boundless: The Official Anthology of the Rio Grande Valley International Poetry Festival, Mundo Zurdo 8, Anacua Literary Arts Journal,* and *riverSedge.*

DEDICATION

For my familias,
the one linked by blood,
and the one linked by love.

CONTENTS

under the sun

el mundo......3

abecedarian for borderland ghosts......4

a memory of fair park......5

prayer to the gulf of mexico......6

waiting for the bus at the central de autobuses in mcallen, texas......7

masquerade......8

games played under soapberry trees......9

cloudwatching......11

merienda......12

vuelo......13

isabel......14

for pit and skin......15

hummingbirds......16

lola, or lala, or lupe......17

learning to swim......18

making sugar in alamo, texas......20

how to pick tortillas off a hot comal......22

calling home......23

self-portrait of the poet as a christmas ornament in downtown mcallen, texas......24

escombro......25

when the drought ended......26

to the man sitting across from us at the hospital in harlingen, texas......27

under the moon

swallowing......31

running with a river on my left......32

finding rasquache......33

prayer to the corn moon......36

mother never talks about death......37

when the figurine of la virgen fell......39

blood moon......40

the first migration of the mariposa......41

the last migration of the mariposa......42

how to play it safe at a texas bbq: a joto's guide......43

devil birds......45

brunch with eggs and fangs......46

to kiss a monster......47

in medias res......48

a poem written in the time of lurkers and stalkers......49

-ito......50

crosswalk......51

i in wind......52

ghost flower......53

river escucha......54

not the shadow but the specter......55

a little browner......56

how to write a poem in the time of swine......59

notes from my hood in the time of covid-19......60

trypophobia......62

american mathematics......63

3rd to last exhalation [which means it will go untouched]......65

songs from a raw throat......66

sugar skull......68

UNDER THE SUN

el mundo

from an early age I was told
flowers and florals
were for girls

I liked them anyway
my eyes secretly tracing
roses, hyacinths, sunflowers
blooming on mamá's blouses
buela's skirts

when we played lotería
I was expected to like La Sirena

the roundness of breasts rendered on cardboard
should've lured me
into the depths of manhood

I liked El Mundo instead

his chest wide, his back ample
the world balancing on the mounds of his shoulders
the authority of his thighs governing my gaze

when I played outside
I was taught
birds were supposed to be shot
with a sling, a rock, or a BB gun

I preferred to watch them hop
from branch to branch
hoping they would turn to me and say

we know you, florecita,
we know you

abecedarian for borderland ghosts

around 6 am
buttressed by the indigo
cool of dawn
did you feel the leap

everyone soaring over
fields like rows of black feathers
grieving for the other
how they hunger to be solid

inside each you could pry open the wind
jawed like a hyena
knead an oracle of teeth
let the light be done

mark this a game of truth
not yet a hallowing
ornament of bruises
praying along the horizon

¿quien nos busca?
remembrance and olvido
shuffle a claim of constellations
"tú mi otro yo"

under the loam
voluted accents
wait for the fresh
x heralding the new cycle

ya viene el nuevo amanecer
zapateando

a memory of fair park

loud and feral the hunger for horizon
bisects the hood
in the belly of a freight train
howling a smoky fuck you

to church bells
& political signs of millionaires
toothy like bobbing milkweed
in the morning fog

which way to the cemetery
which way to the mall
which way to the seagull

cries, the mother & her children
at the crossing cross
not a saint in sight

prayer to the gulf of mexico

                                eye
                        lip
                    throat

    thousand-toothed jaguar
 kisser of forked river-tongues

rio grande
 rio bravo
   boca chica

    spume of wild stanzas
      rustled meters
          dune-grass-verbs

            salt shadow
              wave mother

                list in my ear
                    forgotten names

                        potent names
                            cleansing names

                                charged with vowels
                                    of caracol and corn

waiting for the bus at the central de autobuses in mcallen, texas

        the boy wants to be a cloud   in the next life

                pink nopal   blossoms

a mariposa

      to follow   the gulf coast
                        breeze   he wants to be

    a crossroad   a circumference
                                of twine the kind
              that sheds

of himself
      a draft
         of wind   the winding

   himself   the rushing
          through   mesquite thickets

him   self

 an oxbow lake arc
late october's rim
    that is a creek
       that is a moth
          that is a wing
             that is a storm
               that is   a lengua
               a chicharra
          chant spiral   cresting

        whippoorwill   calls

      ball lightning
    the amber   healing of copal smoke

   the caliche trail   home

masquerade

everyone is a river
or a mirror shard
the shimmer at least

oh how we play it off
fingers a steeple of bones
ready to waive a scar

how many would gnaw
the flagpole's bitter root
if it meant flying like a knife - a bullet

every man for his own
myth and monolith anchored
around their collar

every woman forsaking
her mask as the word
abuse crawls up the aisle

games played under soapberry trees

1.
god's judgement tumbles
like lincoln-log-children
down imaginary ravines

the comedy
is in the hymns
we sing as they fall

2.
feed scabs and blood to ant lions
grow them
into monstrous scorpions

train them to sting
playground bullies
who live to pinch your nose
and fill your mouth
with the taste of copper
in the balls

3.
sister insists
we excavate
to cicatriz

describes a city of scars
a wound, a moaning entombed
beneath our rusty feet

her belly pressed
against the swing's seat
she hovers inches above packed dirt

her pink fingers frantic
to save every woman unearthed

she feeds them seeds

4.
we spin and reach
for the horned moon's carapace
slicing a sickle dream-bridge

across the sky
scrape our clay-coated tongue
against the plum pit of dusk

the hubris of play synchronized
like tethered stars

cloud watching

```
L A Y A C R O S S G R E E
N J A G U A R S H A D O
W S E R P E N T D R E A
M F A N G S S K I N H E A
T W A V E F R A C T A L
R I V E R B E D Q U I C K
S I L V E R C U M U L O N
I M B U S A U B A D E E S
C A P E E D G E R E F U G
E E S S P I N E J U G U L
A R T H R O A T T E N D
O N S S C A R S F L O A T
```

merienda

we devour god
in this pan dulce house
dressed in rainbow crumbs

heaven's ample sunrises
could never be
this sure and honest

here a hummingbird
can dream of being king
crowned with a circlet of roots

come children of unmapped roads
through breaches and wall cracks
up onto lapis thrones

leave behind the fly-bitten rind
laugh at the moss-covered fools
swallowed by their own thicket of thorns

vuelo

you never wanted me
to leave

this valle
of recuerdos

taught me to flesh
roots over ancestral bones

but i've harvested
peregrine wings
where you planted shunning

and when the river's hunger abates
you will see

how i catch
the tail end of a thunderhead

how i soar

isabel

i wish i had never called you mojada
that first day you walked into our classroom

it was an act of self-preservation
i was eight
you must understand

you were new and brown like me
and i was tired of being called mojado
by other kids too

i wish i had never said your hair stunk
of moldy tortillas and sour lard
single-filed against the white-washed bricks
of crockett's cafeteria

i knew you heard me
when everyone cackled
as you ran from the line

all i wanted was to own
a blue "good citizen" ribbon
to please the misses and the misters
who wanted us to stop
smelling like onion fields and diesel
and speaking "mexican"

i wish i had never told the class you'd peed yourself
that's what i thought mojada meant
i was only eight
you must understand

and mrs. torres never taught us
how it was a bad word

for pit and skin

the leaves of the avocado tree
in grandmother's yard prattled
when the wind gusted
like water over river stones

on snarling august days
i'd escape the throttle of the house
and eat mangos under it
let the cool juices dribble down my fingers

what lips and tongue missed
i'd let fall
onto the cobblestones
where the sun laughed in slices

in the shade i held funerals
for pit and skin
sealed by prayers of black earth

here lies a good fruit

hummingbirds

sister and i ate boiled ebony seed pods
            the summer of cat's claw and yucca thickets

                      diagraming names
                          of future lovers
                                  threaded

                      through chain-link fences

      each   a constellation of open windows

      the lavender sunset
   called us hummingbirds

lola, or lala, or lupe

the first horse i saw was an old mare named lola, or lala, or lupe. i was nine.
i remember my uncles elbowing each other and laughing when they said her name,
the way men do when shame comes cinched with pride.

i had only seen horses in westerns, old gladiator classics like ben hur, and war dramas
grandpa liked. the lead man's horse always majestic, grand,
and given extra screen time if it fell in brave service to the cause.

the rest blurred
at best rushed regally with a purpose across the screen. their eyes wide,
their noses flared like lacquered stallions racing around livestock show carousels.

lupe, or lola, or lala was not one of those magnificent steeds.
she plodded along the ranch's wooden fence,
heavy eyes searching for something green among the dry weeds snapping by her feet.

her head dropping low into the taller tufts
at the sound of my uncles' roars as if to muffle their stories
about women's behinds, and hips, and mounting. and her name,

muddied in their beer-smelling mouths full of cracked-corn-teeth
and slurring tongues that matched the technicolor sunset
i wanted her to reach.

learning to swim

i'm 5. grandpa buys me a yellow raincoat like the one's white kids on television wear, so i don't get wet walking to school. it's itchy, hot, and smells like a rubber glove and i have no choice but to wear it.

i'm 33. i blame alcohol and myself for my boyfriend's hands around my throat after leaving juan's party early because i had a fever. *he does it because he loves me*, i tell myself before i pass out.

i'm 8. i fracture my tibia in the playground of primera iglesia bautista of harlingen after being told not to play outside because sleet had made everything slippery. my leg is bound tight in dad's old shirts when we get home. there's no money for doctors or hospitals.

i'm 21. i hear a woman holler by the canal behind crockett elementary. maybe it's just aunt chana looking for her cats. maybe it's la llorona coming to take me for touching charly's penis when we were 10.

i'm 13. i pray for grandma to wake from her coma —it's the last time i pray.

i'm 17. i develop a crush on navy recruiter rios who comes to the house every saturday of april. he brings brochures and success stories of other barrio guys who joined the ranks and now own houses and drive brand new cars after four years of "traveling" the world after high school.

i'm 7. mamá, sister, brother and i hide in the closet during a lightning storm that downs a mesquite in the neighbor's yard.

i'm 12. i stone the one-eyed grackle pecking at the figs on grandma's tree. she loves figs and birds. i never tell her what i did.

i'm 41. mother sobs against my chest and asks if she's been a bad mother.

i'm 35. i almost drown pulling my brother out from the deep end of the pool. we are learning to swim.

i'm 37. i visit the border wall in hidalgo, texas 15 miles from my apartment as if it is a tourist attraction in another country. its rusty beams trace an aura of blood in the sky. i can smell and taste the iron when i close my eyes at night.

i'm 46. i forgive myself for crying like a child every time i hear the finale of stravinsky's firebird.

making sugar in alamo, texas

the old man sets fire to sugarcane fields
on still august mornings
that's his job

                                    "sugar is brown until bleached"
                                    he tells me over gas-station breakfast tacos

at sunrise his evacuation warning booms
from loudspeakers mounted on the roof of his F-150
into acres of green stalks taller than us
en español and inglés

                                    "unprocessed sugar is healthier for you
                                    anyway" he says

some days tired feet are escorted
into white vans
lined up on the road's shoulder

some days snowy egrets pursue
heartbeat-shaped echoes

some days the cane whistles
hollow bone-shaped hymns
across a horizon of possibilities

                                    "white sugar is the number one killer
                                    in america" he says

at noon the horizon froths
knots of black clouds

                                    "two years ago they found the body of a
                                    man in the field," he tells me
                                    "sheriff said he died
                                    of heat exhaustion or dehydration
                                    god only knows who he was"

at midnight i harvest surnames among feathers of ash
piling against my doorstep
they mouth a litany of roots like a thorny rope
i wrap around my neck

how to pick hot tortillas of a hot comal

i learned from my father to use my nails / to let them graze the hot cast iron plate / to be swift / the nail will only deflect the heat for a red second / less if your fingers are soft / they haven't worked enough

to remove tortillas from a direct flame / you must be quicker / surer of yourself / your fingers / thick skin & calluses help / speed and confidence mark the master tortilla flipper and server

this does not apply to warming tortillas in a microwave / the difference is evident when you bite into one / the fire and the man are missing

calling home

      his words fly south
       past checkpoints
           jaguarundi trails
              cenizo paths

              seeking home   buscando

currents
       snaking behind carrizo walls
            white grulla wings

                  kiskadee songs
                     under retama blossom

sunsets   gathering strips of home
            snagged on barbwire rust

            flor de papel memorias at quinceañeras
                      cempasúchil over altars

                  buganvilias reventando
            amaneceres grises

        his words
          fly south

              his body   en el norte
        con el corazón en la lengua

self-portrait of the poet as a christmas ornament in downtown mcallen, texas

sometimes i wonder if i had been made in the u.s.a would my name still be mispronounced, and would callused fingerprints be imprinted on it instead of a tilde.

on the bottom of a shelf at casa sharon there is a gold plastic bell with a red bow that hasn't sold in five years. i know it's the same bell because year after year my reflection on it never ages. i should buy it. maybe next christmas.

silver milagritos and 24k gold chains sold by the pound at the corner of fresno and 17th.

a homie flashes me a smile and winks at me on the down-low by the hierberia where they sell ojo de venado on red yarn to ward off evil eye and envidia.

santitos, santa muerte, and santa claus with a tasty candy cane in his pocket just for me wait in the alley.

across business 83 i can see the big hotel where they say a woman hung herself and now haunts the place by turning bathroom faucets on and off. nobody can give me her name, but she's been seen on overcast nights looking down from the balcony tower. a silent llorona without a river.

walking down main always makes me hungry and my stomach snarls in unison with the diesel engines of the mexican busses down at the station on 15th and austin. i haven't been inside in a decade, but i remember the tired acrid smell of travel. i watch a bus exit. breaks bellow and wail a holiday tune i can't put a name to but will remember years after it turns the corner, like the wreath on its dusty grill –a butterfly graveyard over white flock that swirls like ashes along the highway, an ofrenda for the desaparecidos, the living, and the dead.

escombro

        i woke up   with a chicharra in my throat

           a bee   in my ear

        wasn't me

                until i washed
                      the escombro

                        of streetlight nightmares

                off the soles of my feet

                            fed the bathtub drain

      swirls   of sirens

           like galactic arms

when the drought ended

we speculated on how
the sky would fold
and dull the blades around our necks

one by one
we licked dewy petals
until we succumbed

to the pleated soil
we sacrificed
our polystyrene tethers

we planted forget-me-nots
burned scorpion effigies
counted kestrels

flying into thunder
we renamed home

to the man sitting across from us at the hospital in harlingen, texas

I know that look
that look
on your face

                                        I know

                                        that glare
                                        from across
                                        the waiting room

I know it isn't
my torn jeans
or my mother's old skirt

                                        you scowl at
                                        with impunity

I know it's our voices
our words
our lengua
sparking

                                        your teeth-grinding
                                        your jaw-locking

so, I enunciate more carefully
I set each syllable on fire

corazón
dolor
cuerpo

                                        your eyes narrow
                                        your mouth fills up

I see

                                        your body shifts
                                        in the chair

I know
what you want to say   you want to tell us

                                      "in America we speak English
in America we don't speak Mexican"

I've heard it before   today
                                you just spit

in our direction

I've seen it before

did you expect me to turn my eyes down?
                                were you surprised when I didn't flinch?

UNDER
THE MOON

swallowing

        i've gathered rattlesnake fangs
            along the spine

          of a river
              too bloody
     to be claimed
as anyone's cradle

  where   olive lizards   commune
                    under sabal palm shade

              where   the sky aches
                        —the burden of saints
                    too heavy

                    and   everywhere
                everywhere

        the swallowing of huizache
    thorns
labeled apple pie

running with a river on my left

at sunset my shadow runs
        eastward down cotton fields
                eastward down rusty sorghum rows
                        staining farm-road shoulders

segments of itself strung
        through sabal palm groves
                & along oxbow lake banks
                        where herons sink their feet

into green water
        it waits for me to catch up
                to pray over swirls of yellow
                        huizache flowers & bags of muddy clothes

the sky a burning scar on our backs
        the gulf of mexico on our forehead

finding rasquache
—for rodney and isaac

the word rolls around my tongue
while i drive out of el valle
and i want to pin it down
put an x in it, or on it, or through it
like rasquaxe, raxquache, or raxquaxe,

but the pickles on the piccadilly raspa
i picked up at the drive-through on 5-mile line
might get stuck on it
so i leave it alone for now
tame it
drive on

cross streets that bend south
towards cracked-mud river banks
mexico
la barda fronteriza like an iron ribcage
fencing northern grey-eyed skies in

i drive east
then west
then east again
rasquache rattles
under the hood of my car
where dad once used a scrapped board
as a spacer in the motor
"nomas por mientras"
 —how long is that

i stop at the pulga in alamo
zigzag around the puestos
search
for the perfect corn in a cup
"preparado bien de aquellas"

find latas de sardinas for dad
and chucherías made to look
like brand-name toys for the nephews
under the same techo
where mr. chivo y su banda
will play after the sun sets
until everyone's shoes are covered
in polvo, recuerdos,
or midnight

before weaving my way out
i pick up a copy of the new star wars movie
yes, the one playing at the theater
and a pixies cd with a black and white photocopy cover
to replace the one that got stolen
last year at the rest stop
past the falfurias checkpoint

today on my way norte
20 cameras will capture
the exact moment i clear my throat
before the agent whose last name
reminds me of desert flowers
asks for my origin and destination
and i will want to answer

> "i'm from over there
> while i point to a huizache in the campo
> and from over there
> pointin g to the yuccas crowning the east
> and from those mountains to the south you can't see
> but can feel in your bones
> and from here
> like the herons and malachites
> that glide back and forth
> above the river you call border every day"

or maybe say

"to a conference where i will explain
'rasquache aesthetics' to a handful of people
who have known it all their lives
like you, like me"

or

"i just want to see how far north
rasquache goes
before it turns
into 'do it yourself' or 'recycled arts and crafts'"

instead i will give him
a safe answer

"san antonio, san marcos, houston"

because x never marks the spot
and rasquache is just por mientras

prayer to the corn moon

for the milk-toothed chamaquitos
summoned by a river tide called mother

for the star children stolen
beneath a canopy of chicharra lullabies

on this land of crucibles
an offering of monarch wings

resurrection swirling
up up up

into the purple
brim of dawn

a remolino
blessing

mother never talks about death

she talks of disease instead
over coffee and sweet bread

    —your aunt juana lost a foot
    to diabetes

    —the neighbor from across the street
    has stomach cancer

    —sister garza from church
    gets epileptic seizures

she pours me a cup
tells me about herself

    —maybe i have diabetes also
    i like pan dulce too much

    —they will cut off my legs

    —i'm losing weight
    what if the last time i got my blood drawn they gave
    me aids

    —i think i have cancer
    my nails are brittle   my hair is thinning

    —look!
    —¡mira!

i see it

not any disease
but how she walks
slower than last year
from the stove to the table

how each bite of bread she takes
is   measured
how time has settled on her shoulders
like a favorite coat

                    —¿mas café?
                    —¿pan?
                    she asks

                    —el café es bueno
                    it cleans your sangre and your kidneys
                    so you don't get stones

                    —no, don't eat too much bread
                    you will get diabetes
                    like juana

i smile and swallow
the aches in my bones
the night sweats
the blood tests
the corpse-weight of waiting

when the figurine of la virgen fell

i was on the couch watching a true-crime documentary
someone shot a white woman
the bruising gaze of her neighbors and cops
aimed at the handyman

el centroamericano
my mother shook her head
in disagreement on the recliner like a broken metronome
a congregation of pill bottles on her side table

la virgen's leap of faith chased the awkward moment
the husband was named the killer
the sanababitches always do it for the insurance
mother said

she was right & we glued the virgen's head back on her body
this time with her chin pointing up

blood moon

the night of the blood moon i eat a bowl of charro beans and share a beer with mama. they aren't home-made. she bought them earlier at the corner taqueria. they are too salty, and the cilantro has lost its bitter green punch, but they go well with the cold bud lite. it's been years since she's prepared her own frijolitos. i know it isn't that the stove doesn't work, as she insists, but the lack of helping hands that moved away; hands that once helped clean the beans of stray pebbles, hands that picked out the best looking ones, hands that helped slice salted pork fat into slippery squares, that chopped onions, tomatoes, and fresh cilantro, that held up steamy spoons of thick broth to eager mouths while she watched.

sitting across from me at the table she tells me my beard is getting too long and laughs when i tell her i want to look like the figurine of san josé in her nativity.

"hoy hay luna de sangre," i tell her by the screen door before leaving.
"si," she answers, "y la luna todo lo ve."

the first migration of the mariposa

he calls me "loco"
i believe

because love always slants   true
like chrome in sunlight   right?

all i want is blood orange
slices after lovemaking

a nectarine trail
leading out through guilty groves

        but fleetwood mac is on repeat
           and "players only love you
               when they're playing"

                    the healing
                       later

                            under streetlamps
                              speeding

                                    into coyote
                              canyons like maws

the last migration of the mariposa

                                                  the scent of his skin
                                                          rusty

                                                that is what the sun does
                                                to brown boys

               his   the unlocked window
                          under the mesquite
                          my footprint tattooed
                          on the sill
                          – crushed red hibiscus

        his   the cinnamon birthmark that migrated

    north
        con las mariposas

how was i to know
his hawk-feathered name
would permanently stain
my lengua

the spine of promesas
split open   nightly
across empty cans of tecate

how to play it safe at a texas bbq: a joto's guide

1. try to blend in

2. don't be a joto

3. don't wear your madonna or janet concert tee
   Selena, may she rest in peace, may pass but don't risk it

4. shorts must be below the knee unless you are white or have money

5. if it is byob, stick with beer
   nothing imported unless it's dos xx or corona
   nothing from a microbrewery and never ever wine or sangria

6. don't drink too much
   you will need full control of your senses

7. if it is a potluck bbq, leave the humus at home
   canned salsa is acceptable
   guacamole is perfect

8. keep your hands in your pockets
   don't let them do the talking
   if they must come, out grab your crotch occasionally

9. spit off to the side or between your feet occasionally

9.1 (advance technique)
   grab your crotch and spit off to the side at the same time if you can
   —de vez en cuando, it might take some practice

10. be prepared to be uncomfortable

11. be ready to hear all about pussy and tetas and maybe ass
    "women, can't live with them, can't live without 'em, right? ¡pinches viejas!"

12. don't be shy

about exaggerating the size of your dick
it's a power pole, a giant anaconda, a mighty sequoia, the axis of the universe

12. don't be shy
about pissing outside behind a bush, or the side of the house, or the fence
remember how mighty your meat is and don't hide it too much
it's only guys anyway

13. accept the sample piece of carne straight off the grill

14. wipe your hands on your pants or your shorts that go past your knees

15. when they bring out the guns to show off, be the first to want to touch
ask if you can shoot it
imagine yourself clint eastwood, or 007, or any dude in a quentin tarantino film

16. don't say film

17. don't be fooled by the metrosexuals
their manicured hands don't mean they won't punch

18. watch out for those touchy-feely drunks

19. don't stare too long even if they stare back
there's usually one that will grab your ass or rub his crotch against you
maybe even take your hand and put it on his junk
—in a fun joking way of course

20. don't grab back at anything
this could go wrong real quick
safety first

21. don't fall in love

22. leave early if you can

23. don't fall in love

devil birds

they call us devil birds
for daring to claim
the magenta of the evening sky
with the luster of our wings
the iridescence of our songs
loud with my brothers and sisters
congregating on street corners
proud of our feather and drift
elegant as midnight
the rainbow not enough
for our brown and black shine
down the sidewalk and the dance floor

divine in the slant of our strut
resting for a spell under soapberry shade

brunch with eggs and fangs

should i shed layers of skin
delicately
one by one

or all
at once with a boom
leaving galaxies quivering

    "what does it mean to dream
    of growling dogs with golden fangs"
    he asks mid-morning

naked
teasing
the membrane of an egg yolk
with the tip of his toast

*burst

mmmm...

    "my grandmother used to say
    dogs in dreams meant loyal friends
    teeth symbolized truth"

i lie to him

to kiss a monster

you must accept
that light bends
against   the grain

at a certain depth
it becomes

a precipice concealed
                        beneath
a familiar house

but you knew that
like you knew   the heft
                     of house ashes
                     on your tongue

you mustn't blame yourself
who would fault
                        a broken window
                        allowing
                        the wind's lament

in medias res

tenderest location. like on a good piece of steak, the juiciest part, the bloodiest part, where the meat is softest. the weakest point between two points. the point that yields. also the squishiest center, the most sensitive spot, like in a bruise. it's the bullseye on a target. and when the archer hits it, bam, the game is over. it's where the action usually happens in a book or a story. where the plot thickens and gets muddled. no escape in sight for the hero or heroine. it's where the storm grows fiercer. The moment before lightning strikes and the clap of thunder at the stroke of midnight followed by a howling wind heard only in brief outbursts through poorly shuttered windows or thin apartment walls. it's a curious thing, this middle. it can be described by words like internal, midsection, heart, or core. it can also mean average and mediocre – not good enough. it is a paradox too. full of happenings and sometimes devoid of them. it is the eye of the hurricane where everything goes quiet before it pummels your other side again, and again, and again, and again you pray that it stops soon. and it will but not until it's done. it's the nature of the beast. and at some point, in the middle of the night, in the thick silence that follows and is yours alone, you ask yourself why you didn't leave when you had the chance, when it all began.

a poem written in the time of lurkers and stalkers

the offering is always a drink
a smirk bridged and tethered
to the 17 open tabs on your desktop

flattery is compulsory
dead weighted and certain like jingling
pennies in a crow's eye

but the pelvises are always wrong
one thrust into twilight
the other a school of silver minnows

the road to this hell is astroturfed, honey
like a showroom boat
every step through it recorded and lusted

-ito

he calls me mijo
but I'm older than him

chiquito
pero I'm taller than him

seduction by reduction
nomás una probadita

machito
tiernito
chivito

like one of his sons
except I get to feel

his hands
on my waist

his palabritas
on the half-moon of my neck

his heat
against my back-
bone   despacito

poquito a poquito
calladito
pedacito
he thinks I'm incomplete
he's sure of it
he knows it

like his kind knows
how to name sombras
in the dark

crosswalk

                    at the corner of madison
                              n
                            d   l street

              p
    i asked a
              s
              s
              i
              n
    luciéraga

        where are you going, lucecita,
                          n

                    the middle
                  of the night

              all the jars
                    r
                  e full

                                              p
                      into the mouth of a cooing
                                              l
                                              o
                                              m
                                              o

                                        r
                                      he
                                        s
                                        p
                                        o
                                        n
                                        d
                                        e
                                        d

                                  full of mourning
                                  full of morning

i in wind

some days i am
dry heat

making you
gasp

for soul
at nightfall

making you
pray

for cloudbursts
mid-canícula

                                      some days i am sheets
                                          of glassy january

                                                spinning down
                                            vacant backroads

                                               granjeno thorn
                                         skimming your bones

                    i've learned no other
                          shapes

ghost flower

something surviving
in this body yearns for river

water and the hum of green
distilled through a ribcage of mud

i would chastise into wings
the scabs on my back

but who has time for a body
that has forgotten how to be

& taught to tremble
to fold itself

along parched horizons
scored with iron bollards like vertebrae

& strung like supplications
to fixed-jawed angels

their lips of bone
their tongues of thorn

unwilling to invoke
the accents of my name

river escucha
for the desaparecidos

somewhere sagrado corazón   boot kicks water jug   thin green line papel picado water sinking into lizard shadows   into acento rattlesnake fangs   into folded dollar bill prayers clouds crossing the sky   the sky the sky the road somewhere la migra el muro papelito doblado numero de   mamá donde llamo sueño llama milagro bones in bags ¡donde!

somewhere dishwasher carpenter   onion field tomato field repollo field callos mano bota sol la dama toilet scrubber el   orange diablo alacrán ¡cuidado! don't fall asleep on the railroad tracks clean chones   water virgen del chorrito nuevo león tamaulipas somewhere tejas arizona   eighteen-wheeler rio bravo coyote blood moon rio grande heat stroke   sand sand sand agua bendita guadalupe tonantzin llorona checkpoint martyr   saint desaparecido ¿donde estás?

somewhere chile silver   víbora cascabel tenemos sueño hambre calor frio rio piedra ruega there he is there   she is there there there no entiendo papers storm get the girl no hay sangre tierra mira   santa muerte slipping into mud blood mud blood mud blood grito piss coyote howling   no te pierdas hay comida gunshot somewhere drone she didn't stop stinker find the bag   follow the trail perro holy father last night luna estrella cranium plastic sack panties   into grass into water into camioneta door shutting caliche   owl   conejitos   ¿donde están?

not the shadow but the specter

not the specter
but the mouth

not the mouth
the teeth

not the teeth
the throat

not the throat
the hunger

not the hunger
the gluttony

not the gluttony
the famine

not the famine
the war

not the war
the grave

not the grave
the void

not the void
the separation

not the separation
the silence

not the silence
the isolation

not the isolation
the cold

not the cold
the bones

not the bones
but the extinction

a little browner

1.
when she was 10
my cousin brushed
her forearms and neck
with a thick paste
advertised to turn her skin
a shade lighter

it bleached
her forearm hairs
made them shine
like corn silk in the sun
like farrah fawcett's feathered bangs
who she adored on charlie's angels
but not in the magazines
that made her look too tan
too coppery
too brown
like her

2.
at 14 i helped grandpa fix our roof
spent weeks under the texas sun in june
i was beautiful
lean and young

until my resident alien card arrived
the first one with a photo
which i hid from my mother
buried it at the bottom of a drawer

too brown
i was too brown
prieto
"a cockroach"
my white mexican grandmother

would surely say

"this is why you need to marry
a white girl
improve the race."
my uncle would advise

and every day i'd pray
to the blue-eyed jesus
framed in mother's room
"lord i don't ask for much
i don't ask to be a güero,
just make me a little lighter
before school starts"

3.
oh how they love
to render us
as a sea of brown
plot an eye here
a tooth there
like a tropical getaway
like a recipe on pinterest
cinnamon skin
copper skin
toasted skin
almond-shaped eyes
chocolate lips
irises like coffee beans
the wholeness of our faces lost
in the frothing fog
of their imagination

expiring under their dirt
& broken horizons
under their paintbrushes
their keyboards
their pens

how will they imagine us for themselves today?
in the fields or streets?

oh how they love to save us from us
teach us to be supple
to stoop
to wear our fathers' boots
to follow our mothers' bleach-burned voices

       don't stir the pot
       turn the other cheek
       walk away
       be the bigger person
       stay out of the sun

& oh

how good it feels
to finally say ¡basta!

how to write a poem in the time of swine

don't use the word pig
it's too cute
wilbur was a pig
he was terrific, radiant, and humble
babe was good
piglet, kind

avoid the word pork
unless talking about food
served with savory sides
like apple sauce or sweet potatoes
remember, always cook it properly
never eat it raw or bloody

ham is for sandwiches
or radios
you can write about being hamstrung
but that is more about being cut down
which swine will often resort to
in their usual ham-fisted way
at which time the rest of the swine
will want to call it a bad apple
but we all know what it really means

and when the barrel makes excuses
for the rot it houses
it's time to throw the whole thing out

notes from my hood in the time of covid-19

1.
we are told that constantine witnessed a cross
in the heavens above the tiber on the eve of battle, and then christendom
was born.
or was it just a cloud and now children are evil
until their sins have been rinsed down the drain and out into the ocean?

today through my window the gulf of mexico and the laguna madre send
me clouds shaped like babies in the afternoon breeze. some will mature into
war-scarred locusts, some into lavender thunder.

2.
i keep returning
to the trestle and bullet

holes and words
bruising iron and concrete

where condom-flashing preachers
pray into the fog

—let me do unto you

and it never is
about you or them

but the silence
beading on the tips of grass blades
when they leave

3.
standing at my chain-link i hear los tigres blasting
la jaula de oro around the corner of l street and jackson
where chucha and her wild granddaughters lived 20 years ago
in the "nice house" with cement floors that everyone envied

i don't know who lives there now —some guy
his electric blue tricked-out truck gleaming
under the late march sun

like a sunday miracle but today
is tuesday or maybe it's thursday
and it really doesn't matter

because the accordion is cutting
clean methodic lines across the empty

streets and through
 the leafless soapberry trees
that decided to boycott spring

4.
the grackles know
summer
will arrive slanted
on the shoulders of fire

flies and then sugar
ash before green
and knowing they call

the setting sun father
the evening star traitor
the moon's rim survivor
dawn's lip hunger

and those of us left
to witness daybreak
sunflowers

trypophobia

i'm afraid of bleeding out
under halos of stiff-necked streetlamps

                        bang
                                    for the color of my skin

                        bang
                                    for the fork of my tongue

                        bang
                                    for my queer brown hip bone
                                    slicing escapes through alleys

i'm afraid of bleeding out
under halos of stiff-necked streetlamps

                    cops kissing bullet casings
                        like eucharist cups

american mathematics

you wake up to 50+ people shot at a concert in las vegas. the gunman 32 floors above the clang of slot machines and neon. the words "lone wolf," "quiet," and "good neighbor" are used to describe the shooter which means he was probably white. which means people will debate if it was terrorisms or not. which means the nra will send out letters promising politicians more money and letters urging members to stock up on guns and ammo because the gun purge is eminent. and the argument on whether this is an american problem, a gun problem, or a mental health problem or not will continue until the next shooting. maybe math can help us find an answer where words have failed.

use the following data from this mass shooting to answer the questions that follow.

victims	victims vs. other shootings	number of weapons found in suite, two homes, and vehicle
851 injured	9 > orlando	20 ar-15 rifles
422 from gunfire	26 > blacksburg	8 ar-10 rifles
58 dead	30 > newton	1 bolt-action rifle
36 women	32 > sutherland springs	2 revolvers
22 men	35 > killeen	9 semi-automatic pistols.
34 at the scene	41 > parkland	9 shotguns
24 at hospitals	46 > aurora	1,600 rounds of additional ammunition
	49 > charleston	50+ lbs of explosives

questions:
1. total number of casualties at next mass shooting _____.

2. can you figure out where? complete the following sequence:
church, theater, school, dance floor, concert, _____.

3. if 500 units of blood were transfused in the first 24 hours on 600 individuals treated and each unit is approximately a pint, how many gallons were transfused? ____gal.

*bonus point question
how many victims, guns, bullets, and gallons of blood are needed to classify a terrorist, a gun problem? how many to elicit a solution? answer in the form of a ratio. ____

3rd to last exhalation [which means it will go untouched]

if possible [envision]
sirens charging
down a lung branch

                    a bird of prey [pray]
                    compressed
                    into a brass sunrise

                                          against the asphalt [dream]
                                          america's barrel
                                            & muzzle dissolved

songs from a raw throat

1.
say my name
taste gunpowder
on your lips

bear the weight
of a collapsed lung
pleated and concealed
under the root of your tongue

fix the misshapen vowels
dust off the debris
from the r's, the s's, the t's
untangle each syllable before you

exhale

2.
 you cautioned me
about sticks and stones

but never mentioned
the heaviness of invisibility

or the gravitational pull
of room corners

you said keeping quiet
was a virtue
"silence   godly"

"doesn't god make thunder?"
i asked once

before lightning
licked my cheek

3.
weave with me
a voice embracing
prevailing
resilient

safe

from black and blue
lacquered avatars
golden acronyms
and stars

follow the thick red thread
from our lips
down our forearms
into the streets of america

braid it

over chalk-drawn altars mapped on asphalt
over wreaths of marigolds, daisies, lilies
swirled like galaxies
like cicada litanies in august

hold my hand

feel

our sister's fingers
our brother's palm
our father's calluses
our mother's pulse

& when the time comes
you will know
how to tie the mending knot
how to intone the healing song

sugar skull

i am that sugar skull you buy
chalk-outlined

in the aftermath of blue
against brown, ebony, red throated

like hummingbird sheen
peeled off in ribbons

tied around the blind spot
under your golden corn-silk hair

i am that sugar skull you decorate
sterilized by cloudless dog days

dried and polished
by river-flavored santa ana sand storms

thirsting and pressed against concrete
walls, asphalt, iron bars

restless inside target and walmart
sacks half buried outside falfurias, texas

you offer a eucharist of ashes
call me martyr

proclaim yourself witness at the edge of town
my face on your child's face

painted by number
i am that sugar skull you proudly display on halloween

devoid of exit wounds and pesticide scented hair
don't you recognize me, america?

ABOUT THE AUTHOR

CÉSAR L. DE LEÓN

Born in Monterrey, Mexico, César L. de León now lives and works in the Rio Grande Valley of Texas where he is an active participant in the local literary scene. He holds an MFA in creative writing and a graduate certificate in Mexican American Studies from the University of Texas Rio Grande Valley. He is one of four poet-organizers for Poets Against Walls which allows him to further engage with the community through workshops, public readings, and other events centered on social justice and border issues. His work has been published in *Queen Mob's Tea House*, *Pilgrimage*, *The Acentos Review*, *Yellow Chair Review*, *La Bloga*, and the anthologies *Pulse/Pulso: In Remembrance of Orlando*, *Imaniman: Poets Writing in the Anzaldúan Borderlands*, *The Border Crossed Us: An Anthology to End Apartheid*, *Texas Weather Anthology*, and *Boundless: The Official Anthology of the Rio Grande Valley International Poetry Festival* among others. He has received awards from the Texas Intercollegiate Press Association and the Columbia Scholastic Press Association.

CPSIA information can be obtained
at www.ICGtesting.com
Printed in the USA
LVHW011714300322
714725LV00011B/1314